FOCUS ON

ANCIENT GREEKS

ANITA GANERI

SHOOTING STAR PRESS

INTRODUCTION

Among the city-states of Ancient Greece, the seeds of Western civilization were sown. The pioneering advances of the Greeks in science, philosophy, and the arts continue to influence our lives today. *Demokratia*, the concept of allowing ordinary people a say in the running of their town, is a Greek invention. It still forms the basis of many governments today. Even when Greece was taken over by the Roman Empire, it continued to exert a powerful and lasting influence upon European culture. This book aims to give an insight into the fascinating world of Ancient Greece, and includes related information about language and literature, science and math, history, geography, and the arts.

This edition produced in **1994** for
Shooting Star Press Inc
230 Fifth Avenue
Suite 1212
New York, NY 10001

Design	David West Children's Book Design
Designer	Flick Killerby
Series Director	Bibby Whittaker
Editor	Fiona Robertson
Picture Research	Emma Krikler
Illustrators	Peter Kesteven
	Dave Burroughs
	Sergio Momo

© Aladdin Books Ltd 1993

Created and produced by
Aladdin Books Ltd
28 Percy Street
London W1P 9FF

*First published in the
United States in 1993 by*
Gloucester Press

ISBN 1-56924-045-0

Printed in Belgium

Geography
The symbol of the planet Earth indicates where geographical facts and activities are included. These sections look at the importance of Mount Olympus to the Ancient Greeks, and at Greek influence in other parts of the world.

Language and literature
An open book symbolizes activities which involve language. These sections explore some of the many myths and legends in Ancient Greece, including that of the fearsome Minotaur. The influence of Greek drama in the theater today is also covered.

Science and math

The microscope symbol shows where science, math, or natural history information is given. Many of the names used today for plants or animals are Greek in origin. Also discussed are the Greeks' advances in medicine.

History

The sign of the scroll and hourglass indicates where historical information is given. These sections look at events in Ancient Greek history, and examine the impact of Greek culture on our society today.

Social history

The symbol of the family shows where information about social history is given. These sections aim to provide an insight into the everyday lives of the Ancient Greeks. Ancient Greek food and clothing are included.

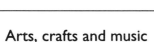

Arts, crafts and music

The symbol of a sheet of music and art tools signals the inclusion of arts, crafts, or music information. Greek architecture has been admired and copied throughout the world. Some of its styles are shown here. The Greeks' love of music is also discussed here.

CONTENTS

THE ISLAND KINGDOM

Greece consists of a mountainous area of mainland and hundreds of islands in the Ionian and Aegean seas. In ancient times it also included colonies in Asia Minor (modern-day Turkey). The first major civilization in this area had developed on the largest island, Crete, by about 2000 B.C. It is called the Minoan civilization, after its legendary ruler, King Minos. The Minoans flourished from 2000-1450 B.C. They traded far and wide and became very wealthy. By about 1450 B.C., however, many of their palaces and towns had been destroyed by earthquakes, and people from the mainland, called Mycenaeans, had taken control of Crete.

Date chart
c.3000-1100 BC The Bronze Age in Crete and Greece. People discover how to mix tin and copper to make bronze for weapons and tools.
c.2600-2000 BC The people of the Cyclades Islands become prosperous.
c.2000-1450 BC Minoan civilization on Crete is at the height of its powers.
c.1900 BC The first Minoan palaces are built.
c.1700 BC The palaces are destroyed by earthquakes and later rebuilt.
c.1450 BC Crete is invaded by the Mycenaeans.
c.1100 BC Mycenaean way of life breaks down.
AD 1894 Sir Arthur Evans discovers the ruins of Knossos.

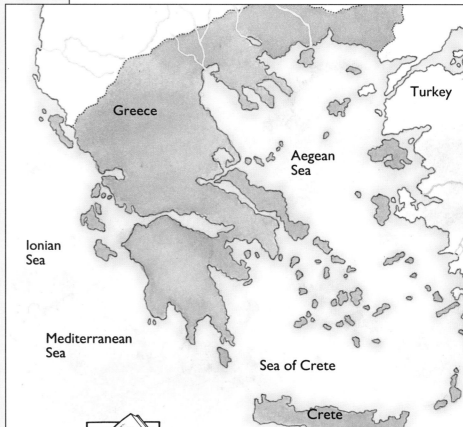

The map above shows the extent of Greek territory during the Minoan Period (in brown).

Main stairway of the Minoan Palace at Knossos

The Minotaur
According to legend, the Minotaur was a terrible monster, half man, half bull, who lived in the labyrinth on Crete. Each year, young girls and boys were thrown into the labyrinth for him to eat. They had no hope of escape because the labyrinth twisted and turned like a maze. The Minotaur was killed by an Athenian prince, Theseus.

Many Minoan towns were built around splendid palaces, such as the one found at Knossos (below). At its height, the palace may have housed thousands of people. It was well organized, with an efficient water supply and drainage system. There were royal apartments, workshops and storehouses. The palace also served as a trading center. Minoan trade was based on wine, grain, and olive oil. Some was stored in the palace; some was exported.

Daedalus and Icarus
In Greek mythology the inventor Daedalus and his son, Icarus, were exiled from the mainland. They fled to Crete where King Minos ordered them to build the labyrinth to house the Minotaur. However, when Daedalus helped Minos' daughter, Ariadne, to escape with Theseus, slayer of the Minotaur (see left), Minos imprisoned both father and son. In an attempt to escape, Daedalus made each of them a pair of wings out of birds' feathers and wax. The wings were successful, and Daedalus flew to freedom. But Icarus flew too close to the sun, the wax melted and he plunged into the sea and drowned.

Palace frescoes
The walls of Knossos were covered in frescoes (paintings done on wet plaster). Only fragments of the originals survive, but they give valuable information about the Minoan lifestyle. The dolphin fresco, shown below, comes from the Queen's apartment.

The bull and the axe
The two main sacred symbols used by the Minoans were a pair of bull's horns and a double-headed axe, called a *labrys*. The bull was sacred to the Minoans. King Minos was thought to have been the son of the god, Zeus, and a princess called Europa. To bring Europa to Crete, Zeus turned into a bull and carried her on his back.

Minoan double axe

MYCENAEAN TO ARCHAIC

The Mycenaeans dominated mainland Greece from 1600-1200 B.C. They lived in small, separate kingdoms, but shared the same language and way of life. The Mycenaeans were great warriors – armor and weapons have been found in Mycenaean graves – and great traders. By 1200 B.C., however, their world had been destroyed by crop failures and economic losses. Greece entered a period of decline, called the Dark Ages, which lasted until about 800 B.C. The Archaic Period, from 800-500 B.C., brought renewed prosperity to Greece.

Date chart
c.1600-1200 BC The Mycenaeans dominate mainland Greece.
c.1250 BC Traditional date for the Trojan War.
c.1100-800 BC The Dark Ages in Greece. The art of writing, known to both the Minoans and the Mycenaeans, is lost.
c.1100 BC The Dorian Greeks come to prominence.
c.800-500 BC The Archaic Period. A new system of writing is adopted.
c.750-550 BC Overcrowding and lack of farmland at home leads many people to leave Greece and establish Greek colonies around the Mediterranean and in Asia Minor.
776 BC The first Olympic Games are held at Olympia.

◼ Greek homeland
◼ Colonies settled

Soldiers on the ramparts defend the palace from attack.

Tomb interior (above)

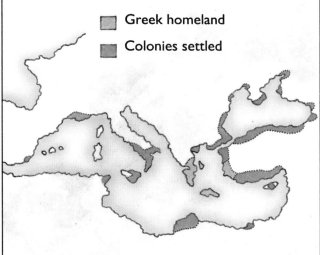

By about 1500 B.C., huge, beehive-shaped tombs (shown above) were being built for the kings of Mycenae. The stones were laid in circles and carefully cut to form a dome. The whole tomb was then covered in earth. Early historians thought that the tombs must be treasuries because they contained so many grave goods.

Grave circle

Excavations of the ruins of Mycenae in the 19th century revealed a graveyard where members of the Mycenaean royal family were buried. The graves were surrounded by a low, circular wall. The Mycenaeans were buried with many possessions. Gold portrait masks (shown top left) were also found in the royal graves.

The early Greeks are called "Mycenaeans" after the greatest of their cities, Mycenae, in the southern part of mainland Greece. Like the Minoans, the Mycenaeans based their cities, and their economy, around palaces. The heavily fortified palace complex was built on top of a hill so that it could be easily defended from attack. This type of city was known as an *acropolis* or "high city." It was surrounded by stone walls 15 feet thick.

The Argonauts

The spirit of travel and adventure in Ancient Greece is reflected in the legend of Jason and the Argonauts. Jason had to fetch the golden fleece from the city of Colchis – a seemingly impossible task – in order to reassert his claim to the throne of Iolchus. He set off in his ship, the *Argo*, with a band of heroes, the Argonauts. They faced many hazards but succeeded in their quest.

The Lion Gate

The Lion Gate was the main entrance to Mycenae. Two huge lions were carved above the gateway. Lions may have been the symbol of the royal family.

Achilles' heel

A person's weak spot is sometimes called his Achilles' heel. In legend, the hero Achilles (see page 17) was dipped into the river of immortality as a baby. He died, however, from a wound to his heel, where his mother had held on to him.

The Trojan War

According to the poet Homer, a Trojan prince called Paris fell in love with Helen, the beautiful wife of the King of Sparta, Menelaus, and carried her off to Troy. The Mycenaeans swore revenge. After a 10 year-long seige, they tricked the Trojans into taking a large wooden horse into the city, unaware that it was full of Mycenaean soldiers.

SOCIETY AND LAW

By 700 B.C., Greece was divided into small, independent city states. Greek society was made up of citizens (men who were born in the city state) and non-citizens (women, foreigners, and slaves). Most city states were governed by an oligarchy – a small group of rich noblemen, called aristocrats. Resentment of their power led to revolts. Tyrants, or absolute rulers, were then appointed to restore order. In 508 B.C., however, a different system called democracy (*demos* = people; *kratos* = rule) was introduced in Athens. It gave all male citizens a say in the government. Other city states soon followed Athens' lead.

A woman's place
In Ancient Greece, women were thought of as non-citizens. Their lives were controlled by men – first their fathers, then their husbands. They could not inherit or own property, or take part in the running of the city. Greek women usually got married when they were about 15. The marriage was arranged and the husband was often much older than his bride. A woman's role in life was to look after the household, spin and weave cloth and raise the children. Spartan women had more freedom and were encouraged to take exercise so that they would have healthy, strong babies. This was frowned on by other Greek societies.

Slaves
Slaves were used as servants or laborers. Some were prisoners of war; others were bought and sold in slave markets. They had no legal rights.

Metics
Metics were people born outside the city state. They were free men, not slaves, and many were very wealthy.

Greek *gymnasia*
In Greece, a *gymnasium* was a center for sport and learning. Apart from training facilities, there might also be a library and lecture hall. In the 4th century B.C., the philosopher Plato and his brilliant pupil, Aristotle, taught in the colonnades of *gymnasia* throughout Athens. Each eventually founded his own school, which became very famous. Plato's school was called the Academy; Aristotle's was called the Lyceum.

Aristotle

There were no lawyers or judges in Ancient Greece. Citizens conducted their own legal cases and trial was by a jury of about 200 citizens. A *kleroteria* used colored balls to pick the jury for the day. Each juror was given two bronze tokens — one for a "guilty" verdict, one for an "innocent" verdict.

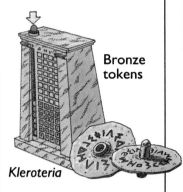

Bronze tokens

Kleroteria

Citizens

Citizens were the most privileged social class in Ancient Greece. Only citizens could take part in the govern-ment of their city state, own land, or speak in a law court. Citizens were also expected to serve in the army.

Changing fashions

Greek fashion changed over the years, although the basic dress for men and women remained a *chiton* (tunic), *himation* (cloak), and leather sandals. There were two basic styles of women's dress. The Doric chiton was wrapped around the body, while the Ionic chiton fastened at intervals across the shoulders. Hair styles also changed. Curly hair (below right) was the fashion during the Hellenistic Period.

An Ionic chiton

Education

In Athens, there were three types of schooling. A teacher called a *grammatistes* taught reading, writing, and arithmetic; a *kitharistes* taught music and poetry; a *paidotribes* taught athletics. A slave called a *paidagogos* was sometimes hired to supervise a boy's education. However, it was only the sons of wealthier citizens who could afford a higher education. Girls were taught domestic duties at home by their mothers.

ATHENS AND SPARTA

Athens and Sparta were the two most powerful city states in Ancient Greece. From about 479-431 B.C., Athens enjoyed a period of great prosperity known as the Golden Age. Science, philosophy and the arts flourished, as did democracy under the statesman Pericles. Sparta, meanwhile, was an oligarchy, led by two kings. There was intense rivalry between Athens and Sparta. This was briefly put aside during the Persian Wars (490-449 B.C.), but revived by the Peloponnesian Wars (431-404 B.C.).

The city of Athens is dominated by the Acropolis hill, with the Parthenon temple complex on the top. In 480 B.C., Athens was destroyed by the Persian army. After the Persians were defeated, Pericles ordered that the city be rebuilt. The Parthenon was constructed between 447-438 B.C. In ancient times, as now, the city of Athens sprawled out at the bottom of the Acropolis (shown right).

Pots of life

Much of our information about the Greeks comes from their pottery. Pots were often decorated with scenes from everyday life and from legend. These tell us about Greek fashion, homes, work, and religion. There were many different sizes, shapes, and styles of pots, depending on their use. *Amphorae*, for example, were used to store oil and wine. Styles of decoration also varied. The Athenian style of pottery, depicting gods and heroes, as well as everyday life (right), was popular from about 500-300 B.C. Greek pots have also provided inspiration for poets such as John Keats (1795-1821) who wrote a poem entitled *Ode on a Grecian Urn.*

Kitchen

Altar

Andron

Workshop

Most Greek houses, like those in Athens, above, were fairly simple buildings of sun-dried mud bricks. The houses of wealthier Greeks were built around a central courtyard where a well provided water. There were separate areas for men and women. Men entertained their friends in the *andron*, which was at the front of the house. Women weaved and chatted in the *gynaeceum,* that was situated toward the rear of the house. Craftsmen often used part of their houses as workshops.

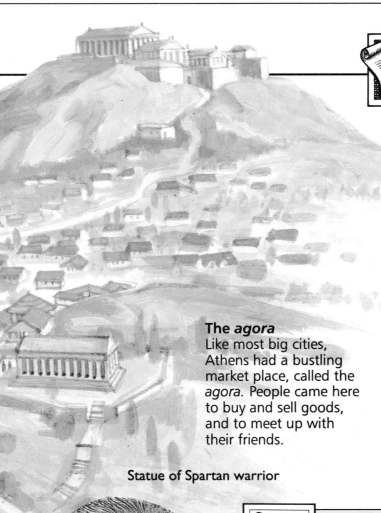

The *agora*
Like most big cities, Athens had a bustling market place, called the *agora*. People came here to buy and sell goods, and to meet up with their friends.

Statue of Spartan warrior

Athens and Athene
According to legend, Athens was named after the goddess of war and wisdom, Athene (below). She beat the sea god, Poseidon, in a contest to see whose name the city would take. Each had to offer something to the city. Athene's gift of an olive tree, providing fruit and oil, was considered more valuable than Poseidon's promise of rich sea trade and so she won. The contest is said to have taken place on top of the acropolis. The temple complex was later built on this special spot and is dedicated to the goddess Athene.

Training Spartan style
Life was very different in Sparta. Every Spartan male had to train to become a soldier. At the age of seven, boys were sent to a military camp. Conditions were harsh and discipline was strict. The boys were kept hungry and had to steal food to make them more cunning. As a result, the Spartans had a reputation for being the toughest warriors in Greece. The Spartans chose such a harsh, disciplined life mainly because they feared that their slaves, the helots, would revolt against them.

Babies were vetted at birth. Weak babies were left to die.

Boys joined the military at the age of 20.

All Spartan girls played sports.

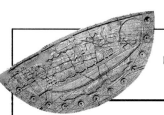

TRADE AND COMMERCE

The warm, dry climate and mountainous countryside of Greece meant that there was a lack of good farmland for growing crops. Although about half the population worked on the land, Greece was not self sufficient in grain or other natural resources. It had to trade olive oil, pottery, and wine for grain, timber, and metal. There was also a widespread slave trade. Traders from each city state and colony sailed all over the Mediterranean in merchant ships, such as the one shown below.

Money
The first coins were made at the end of the 7th century B.C. in Lydia, Asia Minor. The use of coins soon spread to Greece. Each city state minted its own coins. The coins were stamped with the city's emblem, for example an owl for Athens, or with a god or hero, and later with the head of a ruler.

Gold coin from 360-350 B.C.

Coin from Athens, 300-290 B.C.

Coin from Hellenistic Egypt

The map below shows Greece's main trading partners and its major imports. Merchants traded between other countries, the Greek colonies and the city states. The most essential import was grain, much of which came from the Greek colonies around the Black Sea. Athens imported about two thirds of its grain from abroad, paid for with silver from the city's mines. Major exports from Greece included wine, olive oil, and pots.

Shipwreck!

The wreck of a 4th century B.C. Greek merchant ship was found 90 feet underwater near the ancient harbor of Kyrenia, Cyprus. It contained 400 *amphorae* from Rhodes and Samos, and a large cargo of almonds. Archaeologists found the remains of the crew's food - grape pips, garlic, fig seeds, and olive stones. There were also cups, salt pots, wooden spoons, and copper dishes.

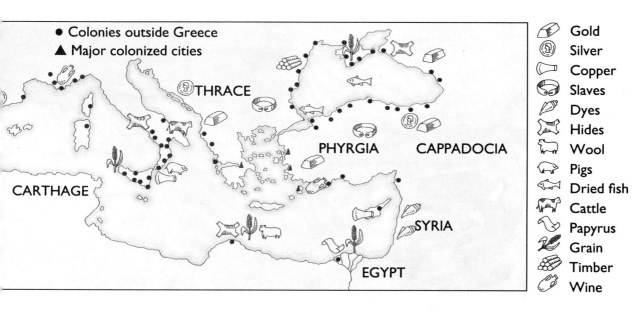

- ● Colonies outside Greece
- ▲ Major colonized cities

THRACE
PHYRGIA
CAPPADOCIA
CARTHAGE
SYRIA
EGYPT

Gold
Silver
Copper
Slaves
Dyes
Hides
Wool
Pigs
Dried fish
Cattle
Papyrus
Grain
Timber
Wine

Weights and measures

In the *agora*, special officials, called *metronomoi*, made sure that the traders used the correct weights and measures and gave people a fair deal. A trader's weights were tested against an official set of weights (like the ones below) to make sure that the trader wasn't cheating. Inspectors, called *agoranomoi*, also acted as quality controllers, checking that the goods sold were of a high enough standard.

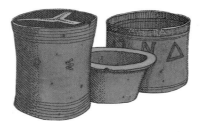

An official set of weights

Greek food

The Ancient Greeks ate fairly simple food – bread and porridge, olives, olive oil, figs, fish, poultry, and cheese. They made cheese from sheep or goat's milk, which they also drank. Wine was their most popular drink. Breakfast might be bread dipped in wine. The foods shown below are similar to those eaten in Ancient Greece.

THE WISDOM OF GREECE

The Ancient Greeks were great scholars and teachers, and many of their ideas and theories still affect our lives today, over 2,000 years later. At first, life and nature were explained in terms of the gods and their actions. By the 6th century B.C., however, people had begun to question the world around them, and to search for more logical ways of making sense of it. These scholars became known as philosophers, which in Greek means "lovers of knowledge." Great advances were also made in medicine, astronomy, geography, history, and math. Modern studies are often based on the pioneering work of the Greeks.

The most important Greek philosophers were Socrates (above) Plato and Aristotle. Socrates (c.469-399 B.C.) taught by questioning his pupils' arguments and exposing weaknesses in them. He was greatly respected by his pupils, who included Plato. But the Athenian authorities were suspicious of his teachings and he was forced to commit suicide. Plato (c.428-347 B.C.) is famous for his works on government (see right). His greatest pupil was Aristotle (384-322 B.C.). Aristotle's works on science and biology were accepted as the authorities on these subjects for over a thousand years. The philosophers and their pupils held heated debates about their ideas, usually in the *gymnasia* (see pages 8/9). The school of philosophers called the Stoics got their name from the columned porch (*stoa*), right, where their founder, Zeno, taught.

Hippocrates and medicine

Asclepius was the Greek god of healing. Sick people prayed to him to cure them. A doctor called Hippocrates (c.460-377 B.C.) adopted a more practical, scientific approach to medicine. Patients were examined and a diagnosis made. Then they were treated with herbal medicines, a special diet or told to rest. Hippocrates wrote about how doctors should behave. Doctors today still follow a code of ethics called the Hippocratic Oath.

The statue, right, of Asclepius comes from the sanctuary of Asclepius at Epidauros.

The study of medicine flourished at the Museum (*Mouseion*) in Alexandria, Egypt, which became the center of Greek scholarship. The study of anatomy was pioneered by a scholar named Herophilus. Another scholar, Erasistratus, made similar advances by studying the circulation of blood in the body, although this was not fully understood until hundreds of years later.

Eureka!

One of the most famous scholars at the Museum in Alexandria was the mathematician Archimedes. His theory of buoyancy, called the Archimedes Principle, occurred to him when he noticed how much water was displaced as he got in the bath. He is said to have jumped out of the bath and rushed out of the house, shouting, *"Eureka! Eureka!"* ("I've got it! I've got it!"). Another of Archimedes' inventions was the Archimedes' screw (below), which is still used to irrigate fields in parts of the world.

Plato's Republic

Plato was a pupil of Socrates. When Socrates died, Plato wrote *The Apology* in defence of his teacher. He also wrote up many of Socrates' ideas in the form of dialogues between teacher and pupil. But Plato is particularly remembered for his work entitled *The Republic*. This looks at ideal forms of government and how they can be achieved. Plato's ideas are still influential today.

Plato and his Academy

Historians

The first Greek historians began writing after the Persian Wars in the 5th century B.C. Herodotus (c. 484-420 B.C.), who is sometimes called the "father of history," wrote about the wars and about his travels to places such as Egypt. Xenophon (c. 430-354 B.C.) had been a commander in the Spartan army. He wrote about the Persian Wars and about the history of Greece. He also wrote a great deal about military tactics and strategy. Thucydides (c. 460-400 B.C.) wrote a history of the Peloponnesian War (see page 10). He relied for information on his own experience of fighting in the war and on interviews he had conducted with other soldiers.

LANGUAGE AND WRITING

The Ancient Greeks all spoke the same language, but different areas had different dialects. In Athens, people spoke a dialect called Attic. When Greek began to be written down, it was mainly written in Attic. The Greek alphabet (shown below) is based on that of the Phoenicians who traded with the Greeks in the 8th century B.C. The Roman alphabet, used in many western European languages, is derived in turn from Greek. Ancient Greek writers produced a great wealth of literature, particularly poetry and drama. Much of this has survived in the form of copies made by the Romans (see page 27).

Greek was first written from right to left like the Phoenician alphabet. Later on, the first line was written from left to right, the second from right to left, the third from left to right and so on. From the 6th century B.C., however, Greek was written from left to right. Use the Greek letters, shown on the right, to write your own name and those of some of the famous Greeks you have read about.

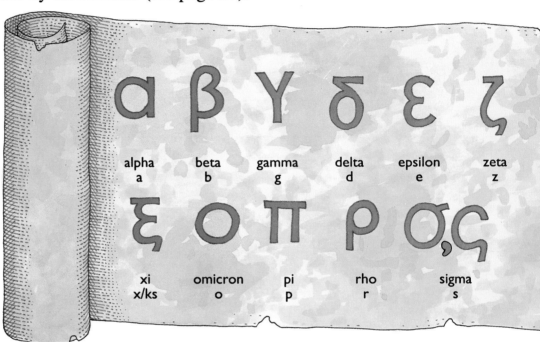

| alpha | beta | gamma | delta | epsilon | zeta |
| a | b | g | d | e | z |

| xi | omicron | pi | rho | sigma |
| x/ks | o | p | r | s |

Early writing

The Minoans on Crete had used a system of writing as early as about 2000 B.C. This was a type of hieroglyphic (picture) writing. By about 1900 B.C., they were using a different type of writing, which is now known as Linear A. Experts have not yet been able to decipher either of these two types of writing. This is mainly because very few examples of the script have survived for people to work on.

Linear A

Math signs

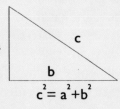

Greek letters are still used as mathematical symbols. The letter π (pi), for example, is used to work out the area or circumference of a circle. π is the ratio of the circumference of a circle to its diameter. The ratio is the same for every circle and has a value about 3.14. The theorems of many Greek mathematicians are still used in geometry, including Pythagoras' theorem on right-angled triangles, below.

Pythagoras' theorem states that the square of the length of the hypotenuse (longest side) is equal to the sum of the squares of the other two sides.

$$c^2 = a^2 + b^2$$

Epic poetry

Two of the most famous examples of Greek literature are the epic poems, *The Iliad* and *The Odyssey*. These long poems were composed by Homer sometime between 850-759 B.C. *The Iliad* chronicles the final stages of the Trojan War and tells of an argument between the hero Achilles and the leader of the Greeks, Agamemnon. *The Odyssey* tells of the many adventures faced by the Greek hero, Odysseus, as he returned home after the war.

A 2nd century A.D. copy of an original 2nd century **B.C.** bust of Homer

eta	theta	iota	kappa	lambda	mu	nu
e	th	i	k	l	m	n

tau	upsilon	phi	chi	psi	omega
t	u	t/ph	ch	ps	o

The Mycenaeans used Linear B (right) from about 1400 B.C. Archaeologists have found clay tablets covered in Linear B among Mycenaean ruins. The Mycenaeans took letters from Linear A and added some of their own to make Linear B. This script was deciphered in the 1950s. It was used mainly to keep records.

Natural names

Many of the words we use come from Ancient Greek. In nature, for example, the name "hippopotamus" comes from two Greek words, *hippos* or "horse", and *potamos* or "river." So a hippopotamus is a "river horse." The rhododendron plant is a "tree of Rhodes" (*dendron* = tree).

DRAMA AND SPORT

The theater and sport played very important roles in the lives of the Ancient Greeks. Men took part in sport not only for fun, but to keep them fit for fighting. Athletic competitions, such as the Olympic Games (see right), were held on a local and national level. The theater in Greece grew out of the songs performed at a religious festival, the *City Dionysia* in Athens. Gradually, the songs developed into plays with several characters, and drama competitions were held to find the best comedies and tragedies. Huge, open-air theaters were built all over Greece.

The actors in a Greek play were men; women were not allowed to appear on stage. They wore masks to indicate the various characters they were playing. To play a different part, an actor simply had to change his mask. Theatergoers were issued with stone tokens which showed them where to sit. The best seats, at the front of the theater, were reserved for the most important people.

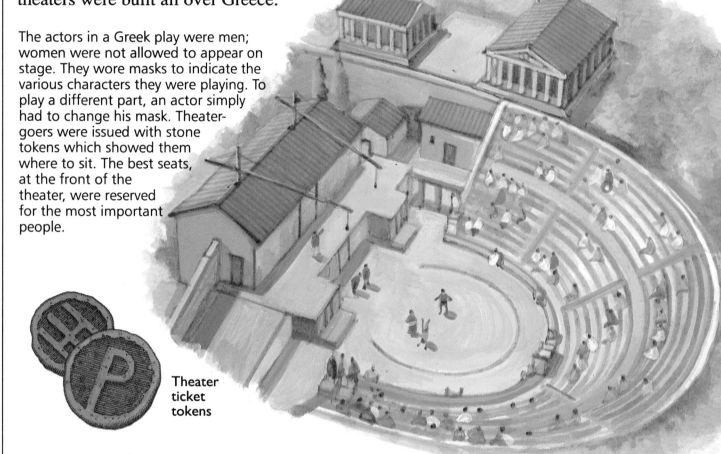

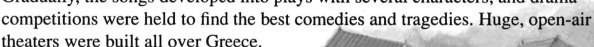
Theater ticket tokens

Musical instruments

Plays and poetry recitals were often accompanied by music. There were also songs for special events, such as births and deaths, marching songs for the army, and songs for religious festivals. Musical instruments included the *kithara*, a type of lyre which was played with a plectrum; a double set of pipes, called *auloi*; and the lyre. According to legend, the lyre was invented by the god Hermes, who made it out of the shell of a tortoise and the horns of an ox.

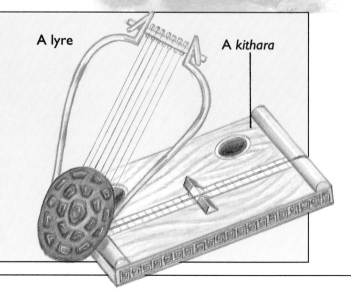
A lyre
A *kithara*

Of the four national sports festivals held in Ancient Greece, the Olympic Games were the oldest and most important. They were held every four years in honor of the god Zeus. The first games took place in 776 B.C. Athletes came from all over Greece to take part in events such as running, wrestling, the pentathlon, and throwing the discus. A truce was called between rival city states so that their athletes could attend. Winning athletes were treated like heroes.

Greek bronze statue from the 6th century B.C. of a Spartan runner

The Olympics today
The first modern Olympic Games were held in Athens in AD 1896, 1,501 years after the last celebration of the ancient games. They were revived by a Frenchman, Baron Pierre de Coubertin, who was inspired by their ideals of sportsmanship. Many of the ancient traditions have been preserved. The modern games open with the lighting of the Olympic Flame. This is lit from a burning torch which has been carried by a team of runners from Olympia in Greece – the site of the ancient games. This ceremony is also reminiscent of the lighting of a fire on an altar by the last runner of the winning team in the ancient games. Athletes from more than 150 countries take part in the games. Winning an Olympic gold medal is a great achievement.

Tragedy strikes
Greek tragedies written by playwrights such as Sophocles, Euripides, and Aeschylus are still performed in theaters all over the world. Almost all of the surviving tragedies are based on myths. According to Aristotle, tragedy had a special aim. This was to take away the audience's own feelings of fear or pity by involving them in the suffering of the play's characters. The main character is usually an admirable, but flawed, person, faced with a difficult moral choice. The play ends with the defeat of the main character by the hostile forces, and with his or her death. This was known as *catharsis*, from the words "to cleanse" or "to clean." Greek tragedies had dramatic episodes performed by a few actors, and choral odes, which a chorus chanted or sang.

Fun and games
Many types of toys and games were popular in Ancient Greece. People played board games similar to checkers and chess, and games of dice. Knucklebones, which was especially popular among women, was played with small animal bones. The Greeks also had a game which was like modern hockey. Children played with yo-yos, hoops, spinning tops, dolls, and balls.

Hockey

Hoop and stick

GODS AND RELIGION

The Ancient Greeks believed in many gods and goddesses who watched over them and controlled what happened in the world. The gods had many human characteristics – they were sometimes angry, or sad, or happy. But they were also immortal and all-powerful and had to be honored and respected. The most important gods were the 12 Olympians (see right). The Greeks built beautiful, elaborate temples for the gods, where sacrifices and offerings were made.

Festivals
Many festivals were held in honor of the gods. One of the biggest was the *Panathenaea* in Athens. It was held every four years and lasted for six days. On the final day, a huge procession made its way up to temples on top of the Acropolis. The worshippers carried a special dress for the statue of Athene.

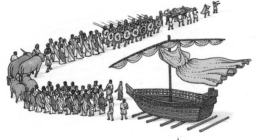

Demeter, goddess of crops and the harvest, sitting on a panther.

The Greeks also worshipped the gods at shrines in their homes. Each day they said prayers at the family altar, which was usually situated in the courtyard of the house. As part of their worship, they poured an offering of wine over the altar (shown right). This offering was known as a *libation*.

A rich person would be buried in a stone coffin called a sarcophagus (below).

Greek coin showing the head of Herakles (above)

Bronze statue of Zeus (left)

Hermes and the infant Dionysus (below)

The gods of Olympus

Zeus Ruler of the gods and of the heavens
Hera Sister and wife of Zeus; goddess of women and marriage
Poseidon Brother of Zeus; god of the sea
Pluto Ruler of the Underworld (Hades); god of the dead and brother of Zeus
Demeter Goddess of crops and the harvest
Aphrodite Goddess of love
Ares God of war
Artemis Goddess of the moon and of hunting
Apollo Twin brother of Artemis; god of the Sun, truth and music
Athene Goddess of war and wisdom; patron goddess of Athens
Hermes Messenger of the gods; patron god of travelers
Hestia Goddess of the hearth; eventually left Olympus
Dionysus God of wine who took Hestia's place on Olympus

Oracles and cults

Before they did anything important, the Greeks liked to know if the gods approved. They might visit a soothsayer to find out what the future held, or ask a priest to read the omens, taken perhaps from the innards of an animal. Sometimes they went to consult an oracle, a shrine where the gods were supposed to speak through special priests or priestesses. The most famous oracle was at Delphi. Here the god Apollo spoke through a priestess, called the Pythia. There were also several mystery cults in Ancient Greece. The most popular was the cult of Demeter and Persephone. Its secret initiation ceremony took place in Eleusis.

Mount Olympus

At 8,750 feet high, Mount Olympus (right), the home of the gods, is the highest mountain in Greece. It is visible from far down in the south of Greece, and from the sea. In ancient times, the gods were believed to live on Olympus in great luxury.

Death and the Underworld

The Greeks believed that the souls of the dead went to the Underworld, or Hades. A coin was placed on a dead person's body to pay Charon, the ferryman, to take his soul over the River Styx, from the land of the living to Hades. The person was then judged according to what sort of life he had led. People who had been very virtuous were sent to the beautiful Elysian Fields. People who had been very bad were sent to Tartarus, a place of eternal punishment. People whose lives fell somewhere in between went to the Asphodel Fields, a dull place where their souls wandered aimlessly.

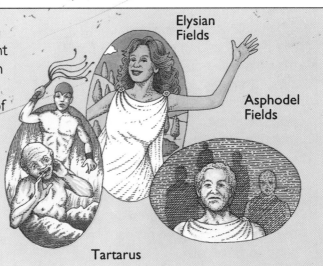

Elysian Fields

Asphodel Fields

Tartarus

CLASSICAL GREECE

The Classical Period in Greece lasted from about 500-336 B.C. Greek culture was at its height, and there was also great military activity. In 490 B.C., the Persians invaded Greece, beginning a series of wars which lasted until 449 B.C. The city states joined forces under the leadership of Athens and Sparta to defeat the Persians. In 431 B.C., however, the Peloponnesian War began. Sparta won the war but both city states were left weak and vulnerable. Sparta was defeated by Thebes in 371 B.C.

The turning point in the Persian Wars was the Athenian victory in the Battle of Salamis in 480 B.C. The Greeks used warships, called *triremes* (above), to ram and sink their enemy's fleet. By the Classical Period, foot soldiers, called *hoplites*, replaced the cavalry as the most important part of the Greek army. *Hoplites* were heavily armed (see right).

Marathon task

The modern marathon race came about as a result of the Battle of Marathon in 490 B.C. Marathon is situated about 24 miles northeast of Athens, and it was here that a Greek army defeated an invading Persian army. According to tradition, the Athenian general, Miltiades, sent a messenger back to Athens with news of their victory. The messenger, Pheidippides, ran the 24 miles to Athens without stopping, and then dropped to the ground, dead. The modern race is just over 26 miles long.

Architectural style

Whereas Greek homes were quite simple in design, public buildings, especially temples, were often very grand. Columns were an important part of classical Greek architecture. Two main styles were used, called Doric and Ionic. Doric columns were sturdy and simple, with plain capitals (tops). Ionic columns were more elegant. Their capitals were decorated with scroll-like designs. In Roman times, a third style, called Corinthian, which was more elaborate, also became popular.

Doric

A *hoplite* wore a bronze helmet, a bronze and leather *cuirass* (back and breast plate), and bronze leg guards. His weapons included a short sword, a long spear and a shield.

Ionic

Corinthian

Forming a phalanx

The most important battle formation in the army was the phalanx (below). This was a rectangular block of hoplites, eight rows deep. In a battle, two opposing phalanxes charged each other until one phalanx gave way. To make the phalanx effective, all the men had to march in unison. If a solider was killed or injured, the man behind stepped forward to take his place.

Date chart

500-336 BC The Classical Period in Greece
490-449 BC The Persian Wars. The Greeks are victorious.
490 BC The Battle of Marathon
480 BC The Battle of Salamis
478 BC Athens and its allies form the Delian League; Sparta and its allies form the Peloponnesian League.
479-431 BC The Golden Age of Athens
431-404 BC The Peloponnesian War between Athens and Sparta (see map below). The Spartans are victorious.
430 BC Outbreak of plague in Athens
371 BC Sparta is defeated by Thebes at the Battle of Leuctra.
363 BC Athens and Sparta defeat the Thebans.

MACEDONIA

THESSALY

Aegean Sea

Persian Empire

Delphi • • Thebes
• Athens

Peloponnese

Peloponnesian War

Athens

Sparta

Neutral states

• Sparta

CRETE

ALEXANDER THE GREAT

As the city states squabbled and fought each other after the Peloponnesian War, the kingdom of Macedonia in the northeast grew more powerful. In 353 B.C., Philip II of Macedonia launched a successful campaign to gain control of Greece. Philip planned to lead a combined army of Greeks and Macedonians against the Persians but he was assassinated in 336 B.C. His son, Alexander, came to the throne. He led the army into Persia, and within 13 years he had conquered a vast empire which stretched from Greece in the west to India in the east.

The racing chariot on this gold coin from Philip II's reign refers to Philip's success in the Olympic Games of 356 B.C.

A gold coin from the reign of Alexander the Great which commemorates the victory at Salamis.

Battle of Issus 333 B.C.

Battle of Gaugamela 331 B.C.

332 B.C. Battle of Tyre

SYRIA

Alexandria 332 B.C.

323 B.C. Alexander dies in Babylon.

KEY

Alexander's route

EGYPT 332 B.C.

Extent of Empire

ARABIA

Philip II came to the throne in 359 B.C. At that time, Macedonia was very poor and split by political differences. Over the next 25 years, Philip reorganized the army into a tough fighting force, united Macedonia and transformed it into the greatest power of the day. Greek independence ended in 338 B.C. when they were defeated by Macedonia at the Battle of Chaeronea.

Alexander's empire was larger than any previous ancient empire, a third bigger than even the mighty Roman Empire. Alexander defeated the Persians in 333-331 B.C. By 326 B.C., he had reached north-west India but was forced to turn back by his battle-weary army.

Philip's tomb
In 1977, over 2,000 years since his death, Philip's tomb was discovered in the royal graveyard at Vergina, Macedonia. His cremated remains were found in a gold casket. Experts were sure it was Philip because the skull had a hole near the right eye socket. Philip had been hit in his right eye by an arrow.

Gold casket

Bust of Alexander the Great

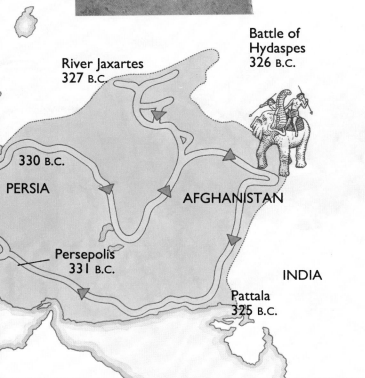

River Jaxartes
327 B.C.

Battle of
Hydaspes
326 B.C.

330 B.C.

PERSIA

AFGHANISTAN

Persepolis
331 B.C.

INDIA

Pattala
325 B.C.

A town called Alex
Alexander founded many new cities throughout his empire. He called all of these "Alexandria." The most famous Alexandria was in Egypt. Under Ptolemy, Alexander's successor in Egypt, it became the country's capital. Its great marble lighthouse, the Pharos (right) was one of the seven wonders of the world.

Alexander wanted the people he conquered to feel part of the empire and not to resent their Greek rulers. To strengthen the ties between the Persians and the Greeks, Alexander took to wearing Persian dress, and married a Persian princess, Roxane. He tried to persuade his soldiers to marry Persian wives. He also wanted the Persians to take part in the government of the empire and in the army. Alexander was a great leader who was respected by his soldiers because he marched as far and as hard as they did. When Alexander died of a fever in Babylon in 323 B.C., the empire was left in a state of chaos and uncertainty.

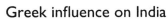

Greek influence on India
As Alexander's empire spread, so too did Greek culture, ideas, and style. They continued to influence the places conquered by Alexander long after his death. In India, Greek styles influenced art and sculpture (below), especially in the region known as Gandhara, in north-west India. Statues were carved with flowing robes, similar to those which appeared on Greek statues.

Persepolis palace
The ruins of the ancient city of Persepolis lie near Shiraz in modern-day Iran. Persepolis was one of the greatest cities of the Persian Empire. It was founded in 518 B.C. by Darius I. During his reign, a splendid palace was built at Persepolis. Each year, festivities were held at the palace to celebrate the religious holiday of the New Year. At these festivities, the king would renew his divine right as king, and would receive gifts from representatives of all the peoples within the Persian Empire. When Alexander captured the city in 331 B.C., he burnt the palace to the ground.

THE END OF AN ERA

When Alexander died, his baby son and half brother were appointed as his heirs. However, the real power lay in the hands of his generals, the *Diadochi*. Alexander's wife and heirs were murdered, and the *Diadochi* split the empire between them. Seleucus took control of Persia, Antigonas of Macedonia and Ptolemy of Egypt. This period is known as the Hellenistic Period, after the Greek word *Hellene* which means "Greek." By 146 B.C., however, Greece and Macedonia had been conquered by the Romans.

DATE CHART

359 BC Philip II becomes king of Macedonia.
336 BC Philip is assassinated. Alexander becomes king.
333-331 BC Alexander invades and conquers the Persian Empire.
326 BC Alexander reaches India.
323 BC Alexander dies in Babylon.
323-30 BC The Hellenistic Period
323-281 BC The wars of the *Diadochi;* the empire is split into three kingdoms.
147-146 BC Greece and Macedonia become part of the Roman Empire.
64 BC The Seleucid Empire in Persia is conquered by the Romans.
30 BC Egypt, the last Hellenistic kingdom, becomes a Roman province.

Map of Hellenistic world, 281 B.C.

Macedonia

Asia Minor

Persia

Egypt

Many Greek temples were raided by the Romans when they invaded in 147 B.C. They stole statues and other precious works of art.

KEY

☐ Seleucid Empire

■ Ptolemaic Empire

☐ Independent states

■ Antigonid Empire

26

The New Testament

During the Hellenistic Period, a form of Greek called *koine* was spoken all over the areas which Alexander had conquered. Jesus and his disciples spoke Aramaic, a non-Greek language, but their teachings were written down as the New Testament in *koine*.

Ptolemy was the most successful of Alexander's *Diadochi.* He and his successors, the Ptolemaic Dynasty, ruled Egypt from 323-30 B.C. Under the Ptolemies, trade flourished in Egypt and the scholars of Alexandria kept Greek culture very much alive (see page 25). But Egyptian resentment and arguments among the Ptolemies over who should succeed to the throne gradually weakened their position. Cleopatra VII was the last ruler of the dynasty. Despite her efforts to keep Egypt free from Roman rule, it became a Roman province in 30 B.C.

Roman art

Roman artists and architects borrowed many of their ideas from the Greeks. They also made copies of some of the best pieces of Greek sculpture. These have often survived where the originals have been lost. Roman scribes also helped to keep the Greek tradition alive. They copied hundreds of Greek manuscripts, which have become our main source of information about Greek literature.

Byzantium

In the 3rd century A.D., the Roman Empire was divided into two halves – west and east. The Western Empire fell in A.D. 476 but the Eastern Empire, which was heavily influenced by Greek culture, survived until A.D. 1453. It was known as the Byzantine Empire. Its capital city was Constantinople (present-day Istanbul in Turkey). The Christianity practiced in Byzantium formed the basis for the Greek Orthodox Church.

Church of Santa Sophia, Istanbul

THE LEGACY OF GREECE

The heyday of Ancient Greece was some 2,500 years ago. Yet the influence of Ancient Greek politics, philosophy, architecture, and language has remained strong in subsequent civilizations. Many of the Latin phrases we use today have come from Ancient Greece via the Romans. Today, many developed countries use a form of democracy similar to that of the Greeks, and we are constantly reminded of their influence through science, medicine, and math.

The Renaissance
During the Renaissance Period (15th-17th centuries), European writers, artists, sculptors, and architects turned to the craftsmen and scholars of Ancient Greece for inspiration. Examples include Michelangelo, Raphael, Leonardo da Vinci, and William Shakespeare. The French dramatist, Racine, was greatly influenced by the Greek writer, Euripides. Two of Racine's greatest plays are the tragedies, *Andromaque* (Andromache) and *Phèdre* (Phaedra). Andromache was the wife of Hector, a prince of Troy. Phaedra was the daughter of Minos. She married Theseus and tricked him into killing his own son.

The theater today
Many of the Ancient Greek theaters remain remarkably well preserved. The theater shown below is at Dodona in northwest Greece. It was built between 297-272 B.C., and could seat over 14,000 spectators. The horseshoe shape not only offered everyone an equal view of the stage, but also provided excellent acoustics, and forms the basis for our modern day concert halls, theaters and auditoriums. Today, the theater at Dodona has been restored and is used for annual drama festivals.

The three basic styles, or orders, used by the Greeks (see pages 22/23) provide the inspiration for many modern buildings. The column from the building below, in London, can be seen to use the Ionic style of decoration.

Persephone and Hades banqueting in the Underworld (right)

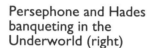

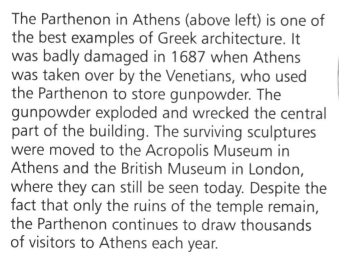

A mythical legacy

Many events were explained by the Ancient Greeks in terms of myths and the gods. For example, an explanation of the world's seasons can be found in the tale of Persephone, daughter of Demeter (see pages 20/21). Persephone was kidnapped by Hades, God of the Underworld. Desolate, Demeter searched the Earth for her daughter, allowing the Earth to become barren. Hades was eventually persuaded to return Persephone to Earth, but only for six months of the year. Persephone's six months on Earth herald spring and summer, while her six months in the Underworld reflect Demeter's despair, and become winter and autumn. Today we have scientific theories to explain why certain things happen. Yet Greek myths remain a powerful source of inspiration for architecture, literature, painting, and music. Many of the stars, constellations, and galaxies (shown below) also have names derived from Greek mythology.

The Parthenon in Athens (above left) is one of the best examples of Greek architecture. It was badly damaged in 1687 when Athens was taken over by the Venetians, who used the Parthenon to store gunpowder. The gunpowder exploded and wrecked the central part of the building. The surviving sculptures were moved to the Acropolis Museum in Athens and the British Museum in London, where they can still be seen today. Despite the fact that only the ruins of the temple remain, the Parthenon continues to draw thousands of visitors to Athens each year.

c.3000-1000 BC The Bronze Age.

c.2100 Arrival of the first Greek-speaking people in the area now known as Greece.

1900 First Cretan palaces are built. Beginning of the Minoan civilization on Crete.

c.1700 Cretan palaces are destroyed by earthquakes and later rebuilt.

c.1600 Rise of the Mycenaean culture.

c.1450 Cretan palaces are destroyed. Mycenaeans take over the palace at Knossos and rebuild it.

c.1400 Knossos burns down and is not rebuilt.

c.1100-800 The Dark Ages. The Mycenaean way of life breaks down.

c.800-500 The Archaic Period

776 First Olympic Games held

c.750-550 Greek colonies founded around the Mediterranean

c.650 The first tyrants seize power on the mainland city states. First coins used in Lydia

c.550 Tyrannies in the Greek colonies

c.500-336 The Classical Age

490 Persians invade the mainland, and are defeated at the Battle of Marathon.

480 Battles of Thermopylae and Salamis

479 Battle of Plataea. Persians driven out of Greece.

431-404 The Peloponnesian War between Athens and Sparta. Sparta wins.

359 Philip II becomes king of Macedonia

340 Greek states form the Hellenic League against Philip

338 Philip defeats Hellenic League at the Battle of Chaeronea and becomes ruler of Greece. Greek states lose their battle for independence against the Macedonians

336 Death of Philip. Succeeded by Alexander

323 Death of Alexander

323-30 The Hellenistic Period

8000 B.C.

First hieroglyphs (picture writing) in Egypt c.3400 B.C.

Old Kingdom in Egypt 2628-2181 B.C.

Pyramids built in Egypt during Old Kingdom

Egyptian Middle Kingdom 2040-1640 B.C.

2000 B.C.

Tutankhamen – the boy pharaoh 1361-1352 B.C.

New Kingdom in Egypt 1552 1085 B.C.

Romulus and Remus found the city of Rome 753 B.C.

500 B.C.

Roman Empire c.27 B.C.-C.A.D. 476

Julius Caesar murdered 44 B.C.

Fall of the Roman Empire A.D. 476

Viking raids on Britain and France A.D. 793-1000

A.D. 1000

First Crusade to recapture Holy Land from Muslims A.D. 1096

First mechanical clock developed A.D. 1350

The Aztec Empire in Central America A.D. 1300-1521

A.D. 1350-1532 Growth of the Inca Empire in South America

8350-5400 B.C.
First cities – Jericho and Catal Hūyūk

3500-3000 B.C.
Wheel invented by the Sumerians

2500-1500 B.C.
Rise of the Indus Valley civilization

Early Minoan period in Crete begins c.2500 B.C.

Stonehenge completed in England c.1500 B.C.

The destruction of Knossos in Crete c.1450. End of the Minoan period

c.563 B.C. Life of Gautama the Buddha

c.1500-1027 B.C. Shang dynasty in China.

Birth of Confucius 551 B.C.

The Golden Age of Greece 479-431 B.C.

Alexander the Great conquers Persia, Syria and Egypt 332 B.C.

The first Empire in China 221 B.C.-A.D. 618

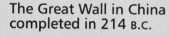

The Great Wall in China completed in 214 B.C.

Samurai warriors of Japan from A.D. 1100-1868

The Plague, or Black Death, spread throughout Europe A.D. 1351

First mechanical printing press developed by Gutenberg in Germany in A.D. 1454

Christopher Columbus sets sail for the West Indies in 1492 and becomes the first European to discover America

GLOSSARY

Acropolis A fortified city which was built on a hill or a piece of high ground. It means "high city" in Greek.

Agora The market and meeting place in the center of a Greek city.

Amphora A large, two-handled pot used for storing wine or olive oil.

Andron A dining room in a private house used by men only.

Attic The dialect spoken by people in and around Athens.

Democracy A system of government in which all citizens could have a say.

Diadochi The "successors," or generals who split Alexander the Great's empire between them when he died.

Gynaeceum The women's rooms in a private house.

Labrys The double-headed axe which was a sacred symbol of the Minoans.

Libation An offering of wine poured over an altar during worship of the gods.

Metic A foreigner living in a city state.

Minoan The name given to the civilization which flourished on Crete from about 2200-1450 B.C. The name is taken from a legendary king, Minos.

Minotaur In legend, a monster who was half-man, half-bull and lived in the labyrinth on Crete.

Mycenaean The name given to the people who dominated mainland Greece from about 1600-1200 B.C.

Oligarchy A system of government in which a small group of people hold power.

Oracle A shrine where people could consult a god or goddess who spoke to them through a priest or priestess.

Phalanx A battle formation in which soldiers are arranged in a block.

Trireme A Greek warship which had three rows of oars.

Tyrant A ruler with absolute power.

INDEX

Photographic Credits:
All the pictures in this book are from C.M. Dixon Photo Resources apart from pages: front cover top, 15 top: Spectrum Colour Library; front cover bottom, 3 middle, 13: Roger Vlitos; 16 top: Robert Harding Picture Library; 19 right, 22 bottom left: Frank Spooner Pictures.